W9-CZK-855

- CUSTOM -
VWs
BEETLES, BUGS, KIT CARS & BUGGIES
A Colour Family Album Special

Dedication
To Raoul and Hilde. May life be kind to you both.

Other Veloce publications -

Colour Family Album Series
Bubblecars & Microcars by Andrea & David Sparrow
Bubblecars & Microcars, More by Andrea & David Sparrow
Citroën 2CV by Andrea & David Sparrow
Citroën DS by Andrea & David Sparrow
Fiat & Abarth 500 & 600 by Andrea & David Sparrow
Lambretta by Andrea & David Sparrow
Mini & Mini Cooper by Andrea & David Sparrow
Scooters, Motor by Andrea & David Sparrow
Vespa by Andrea & David Sparrow
VW, Custom Beetles, Bugs & Buggies by Andrea & David Sparrow
VW Beetle by Andrea & David Sparrow
VW Bus, Camper, Van & Pick-up by Andrea & David Sparrow

SpeedPro Series
Camshafts & Camshaft Timing for High Performance Engines by Des Hammill
How to Blueprint & Build a 4-Cylinder Engine Short Block for High Performance by Des Hammill
How to Build a V8 Engine Short Block for High Performance by Des Hammill
How to Build & Modify Sportscar & Kitcar Suspension & Brakes for Road & Track by Des Hammill
How to Build & Power Tune Weber DCOE & Dellorto DHLA Carburetors by Des Hammill
How to Build & Power Tune Harley-Davidson Evolution Engines by Des Hammill
How to Build & Power Tune Distributor-type Ignition Systems by Des Hammill
How to Build, Modify & Power Tune Cylinder Heads by Peter Burgess
How to give your MGB V8 Power by Roger Williams
How to Power Tune BMC/Rover 1275cc A-Series Engines by Des Hammill
How to Power Tune the MGB 4-Cylinder Engine by Peter Burgess
How to Power Tune the MG Midget & Austin-Healey Sprite by Daniel Stapleton
How to Power Tune Alfa Romeo Twin Cam Engines by Jim Kartalamakis
How to Power Tune Ford SOHC 'Pinto' & Sierra Cosworth DOHC Engines by Des Hammill

General
Alfa Romeo Owner's Bible by Pat Braden
Alfa Romeo Modello 8C 2300 by Angela Cherrett
Alfa Romeo Giulia Coupé GT & GTA by John Tipler
Bentley Continental, Corniche & Azure - 1951-1998 by Martin Bennett
British Cars, The Complete Catalogue of 1895-1975 by Culshaw & Horrobin
Bugatti 46/50 - The Big Bugattis by Barrie Price
Bugatti 57 - The Last French Bugatti by Barrie Price
Chrysler 300 - America's Most Powerful Car by Robert Ackerson
Cobra - The Real Thing! by Trevor Legate
Daimler SP250 'Dart' by Brian Long
Datsun Z - from Fairlady to 280Z by Brian Long
Fiat & Abarth 124 Spider & Coupé by John Tipler
Fiat & Abarth 500 & 600 by Malcolm Bobbitt
Ford F100/F150 Pick-up by Robert Ackerson
Grand Prix & F1 Car, Evolution of the by Simon Read
The Lea-Francis Story by Barrie Price
Lola - The Illustrated History (1957-1977) by John Starkey
Lola T70 - The Racing History & Individual Chassis Record New Edition by John Starkey
Making MGs by John Price Williams
Mazda MX5/Miata Enthusiast's Workshop Manual by Rod Grainger & Pete Shoemark
MGA by John Price Williams
Porsche 356 by Brian Long
Porsche 911R, RS & RSR by John Starkey
Porsche 914 & 914-6 by Brian Long
Rolls-Royce Silver Shadow/Bentley T Series Corniche & Camargue by Malcolm Bobbitt
Rolls-Royce Silver Wraith, Dawn & Cloud/Bentley MkVI, R & S Series by Martyn Nutland
Schumi by Ferdi Kraling
Singer Story: Cars, Commercial Vehicles, Bicycles & Motorcycles by Kevin Atkinson
Taxi - the Story of the 'London' Cab by Malcolm Bobbitt
Triumph TR6 by William Kimberley
Triumph Motorcycles & the Meriden Factory by Hughie Hancox
VW Bus, Camper, Van, Pickup by Malcolm Bobbitt
Works Rally Mechanic - Tales of the BMC/BL Works Rally Department by Brian J Moylan

First published in 1998 by Veloce Publishing Plc., 33, Trinity Street, Dorchester DT1 1TT, England. Fax: 01305 268864.

ISBN: 1 901295 04 4/UPC: 36847 00104 9

British Library Cataloguing in Publication Data -
A catalogue record for this book is available from the British Library.

Typesetting (Avant Garde), design and page make-up all by Veloce on AppleMac.
Printed in Hong Kong.

- CUSTOM -
VWs
BEETLES, BUGS, KIT CARS & BUGGIES
A Colour Family Album Special

VELOCE PUBLISHING PLC
PUBLISHERS OF FINE AUTOMOTIVE BOOKS

THANKS

Thanks to all who helped with advice, cars, and their time. Special thanks to Raoul and Hilde Verbeemen, Eva Verbeemen, Vanessa Ramaekers, Gerard Wilke, Etienne Mertens, John Oron, Rudy & Marcolina Bylsma, Bert Wolfink, Gees and Theo de Kramer, Jon Koks, Nick Slootweg, Yves D'Hondt, Wolter Hemeryck, Eric and Marie-José van Uden, Caroline Verhelle, Bert van Tyghen, Corine de Beer, Joris Kastenberg, Peter Cheeseman of Wizard, Bob Daems, Marco Orriens, Nathalie van der Klok, Eddy Nocon, Michel & Casimir Mokosinski, Angelo Parinello, Philip Schreurs, Anita Draelants, Marie-Jeanne Draelants, Fhiloméne Noten, Edd China, Franke Merifield, Geert de Poorter, Marie-Louise Wolfs, Patrick Sanadornoel, Mario & Sandra de Trel, Henk van der Kroef, Jean-Pierre Honings, Jean-Marie Stulens, Maarten Stulens, Peter Schoemans, Johan Quintiens, Geert de Poorter, Donna Chandler, Dennis Terry.

CONTENTS

INTRODUCTION

When we were taking photographs and gathering information for the Colour Family Albums on the Beetle and the Volkswagen Bus, we visited lots of VW events around Europe, and found plenty of beautiful Beetles - original and restored - that perfectly fitted the bill for those books. We also came across a wonderful array of customised Beetles which were just too special to ignore. Some were specific makes of Buggy or Roadster, others individual customisations. The imagination and creativity that had gone into building them, and the attention to detail, were quite remarkable. This cannot always be said of customised cars. Nor can it always be said of marque devotees that purists and customisers live together in perfect harmony: VW owners, however, seem to have found a good balance.

This book does not set out to catalogue every customisation, alteration and addition. Some of these cars are well known; others are not. Some are based on standard customising products, others are the highly individual work of an enthusiastic owner. Some are sophisticated, others downright silly. What they all have in common is the much-loved Beetle as their base.

Bugatti Brescia Type 23 (1925) replica.

WHY CUSTOMISE?

Why would anyone want to take a perfectly good Volkswagen - a down-to-earth, unpretentious, good-looking Volkswagen - and change it? Are there not enough different cars in the world, enough shapes, styles, engines, colours and combinations, to suit every taste? No, there are not. Manufacturers' extensive accessory lists, and the specialist shops selling every conceivable add-on option, from amme-ters to 'zebra' seat covers, testify to the fact that there are as many different ideas of what constitutes the ideal car as there are car owners. Naturally, some people do take things to extremes. Would you cover *your* Beetle in fake fur, or furnish it with a rear door? Would you turn it into a Bugatti lookalike? Or do you aspire to be propelled from 0 to 60mph in six seconds in your personal Bug?

Of course, customising is

A meeting of form and function.

There's nothing cooking in the front of this Ferrariesque creation.

Sides that pay homage to the Ferrari Testarossa ...

... and a rear that echoes the lines of the Porsche 928.

... but the inside is still Beetle-sized.

Red Porsche/Ferrari Beetle

Owner - Andrew Habrahen

- Base model - 1303 S Beetle, 1974
- Engine - Porsche 914 injection
  1700cc, 80bhp

- Exhaust - owner's own concept with 'Laser' pips from Suzuki 1100

- Wheels - Mongels 'Mojoh' chrome
- Tyres - front 195/60/15, rear 235/60/15
- Brakes - original 1303S

Porsche 928 kit from Lincar of the Netherlands, with owner's own concept Ferrari-look. With the exception of the original body, all the parts are polyester. Electric one-piece windows. Porsche 911 dash and front seats. Original 911 Turbo electrio-pneumatic fin driven by compressor under the rear seat.

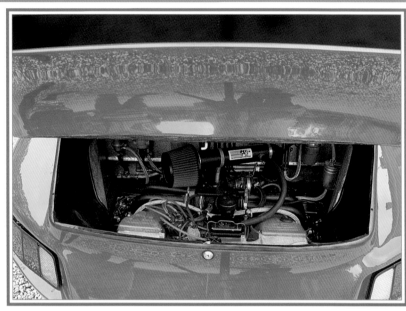

Porsche 914 power.

The Cyrano de Bergerac of the Beetle world?

Built for two - the interior paintwork and detail follow the same colour scheme as the exterior.

nothing new. The very first automobiles were pretty much customised, since the bodywork would be constructed to order on the customer's choice of chassis.

Early preferences might well have been for wood panelling and leather seats, but there were few set specifications, and most things were negotiable. If you wanted to check

on your chauffeur's road-sense from the comfort of your rear seat, you could have an exquisite rear-view mirror fitted, just for that purpose. If you suffered from puncture

paranoia, you could specify extra spare wheels. If you were short and your regular front-seat passenger was tall, you could have individual seats to suit you both.

There are two main categories of customising: performance-based and appearance-based. Some cars will fall neatly into one or other category, although most will overlap to varying degrees. A car with added power may be discreet, with only small aerodynamic touches hinting at what is beneath the hood, or it may shout its abilities with every fin and spoiler - and in chrome lettering on the back for anyone who missed the message. Then again, that flash, road-hugging monster may be so weighed down with automotive jewellery that its poor little engine can barely drag it along. Customising stems from taste: not that indefinable sense that some people claim (which always seems close to snobbery), but the taste that is simply personal preference.

Cars can be a very good medium for self-expression. Houses have some drawbacks in this respect, being shared, perhaps, with other adults, children, dogs and cats; set among other houses, they cannot be painted lime green and pink on a whim. Cars, on the other hand, are ideal. They can impress with impunity, and move on. They can be appreciated completely on their own terms, and on many levels. It is quite possible to admire the most outrageously customised car - quite genuinely - without in any way wishing to own it, drive it, or

construct anything like it.

What, then, of the Volkswagen and, in particular, the Beetle? Why has it proved so popular for customisations of every kind? So many millions of Beetles have been made over the years, of course, that there is always a plentiful supply of donor vehicles for the basics. The fact that the Beetle has a separate chassis means that removing the bodywork is a much easier proposition than is the case with some other cars. Then, there is nothing about the Beetle's intrinsic personality - nothing haughty or proud - to clash with its acquired persona. Simple adornment is quite easily achieved, and if you are handy with those extra skills (welding, chroming, paint-spraying, and so on), or know someone who is, the sky's the limit.

People with a shared love of cars can be very generous with their time and expertise. It is quite usual to find four or five cars that have all been painted by one of the owners, had their engines stripped and rebuilt in another's workshop, and so on. On one occasion, we met a lady with a passion for needlework who had crafted intricate, individualised *appliqué* designs for the seat covers of her own and her friends' cars. Beetle owners are a friendly bunch, and this kind of co-operation occurs naturally within their relationships.

Would Professor Ferdinand Porsche be upset if he could see the changes that have been made to some of his 'people's cars'? Probably not:

13

early in his career the great man did his share of, if not exactly customising, then certainly altering cars to suit particular purposes.

Since his days at the Austrian Daimler company after World War 1, Porsche had cherished the ambition of getting into production a small, economic car for the people. However, it was fifteen years before the foundation stone was laid at the Wolfsburg plant, and another seven before the Beetle went into serious production. The

car notched up amazing production figures: the one million mark was passed in August 1955; five million in December 1961; ten million in September 1965; fifteen million in February 1972, and twenty million in May 1981.

The basic body shape of the Beetle remained unaltered all this time, with major exterior changes being increases in the size and shape of the glass areas, including the windscreen, and modifications to the lights, front and rear. Mechanical changes

tended to be the results of improvements in technology, such as the change to twelve-volt electrics and increases in power output from the engine.

Special editions - sometimes an excuse for customising - sported mainly cosmetic differences. The GT Beetle of 1972 mixed 1300-style bodywork with a 1600 engine (adding flashy wheels for good measure), and, in the same year, the 'Marathon' celebrated the Beetle's breaking of the Ford Model T pro-

A little square box trailer would have been a disappointment; everything on this unit matches the car, from the front ...

... and the rear, including the Frenched lights and the wheel trims.

duction record. Perhaps the most flamboyant was the 'Jeans Beetle' (wearing orange paintwork and denim seats), and the classiest, the understated 'Silver Bug,' in metallic silver with a black stripe and a special logo, celebrating the twenty million production high spot.

But it was the owners who really got to grips with the potential for individual expression offered by the Beetle. As you can see, they do not disappoint!

American-inspired Beetle & Trailer

Owner - Bert Wolfink

- Base model - 1300 Beetle,1975
- Engine - 1700cc single carburettor
- Wheels - 15 inch, front 195, rear 205

Car inspired by 1934 Ford, and individually made by the owner. Body and boot in steel, wings, side skirts and roof hood in Polyester. Finished in an Audi colour. Matching trailer is unusual in matching the car's front and rear styling.

Fabulous lilac/bronze colour alters subtly as the daylight changes.

EARLY DAYS

2

Ferdinand Porsche first conceived the idea of an affordable people's car after World War 1, when times were hard and the need for personal transport was growing. The idea was sound, but remained a dream for another fifteen years: several times Porsche came close to realising his ambition, only to be thwarted by circumstances beyond his control.

However, in 1933, Porsche was called to Berlin to meet Hitler, who wanted to get a small car into production. Porsche was given the task of developing the 'Volkswagen.' Prototypes were built and tested, a scheme was established to help members of the public save up for their car, and a site at Wolfsburg was commandeered for the factory.

By 1944, however, allied bombing had reduced much

Hebmuller was commissioned to develop a cabriolet at the same time as Karmann, but a factory fire destroyed its chances of equal success. (Wizard Hebmuller replica).

of the factory to ruins, and by the time the allied forces arrived in April the following year, there was very little left that could be put to immediate use.

Under British authority, rebuilding began. Dr Heinz Nordhoff was chosen as the man to take over the plant, which he did in 1949. He

Metal-flake paint, in cool greens, blues and mauves - all have been popular choices for the Buggy, and so have bold, bright, plain reds, oranges and yellows.

A good Beetle chassis proves an ideal starting point for so many conversions and customisations. The post-1968 rear light clusters are in perfect proportion for this Buggy, whilst the exhaust system suits it down to the ground.

Transparent engine cover shows off a chromed and polished engine, but keeps the dirt at bay.

Plain colours are always popular; graphics must be bold, bright and unfussy. This Wizard-based Roadster combines the best of both.

Left - One aim is to accentuate the roundness of the original design. Here, this is done with a shield-shaped engine cover.

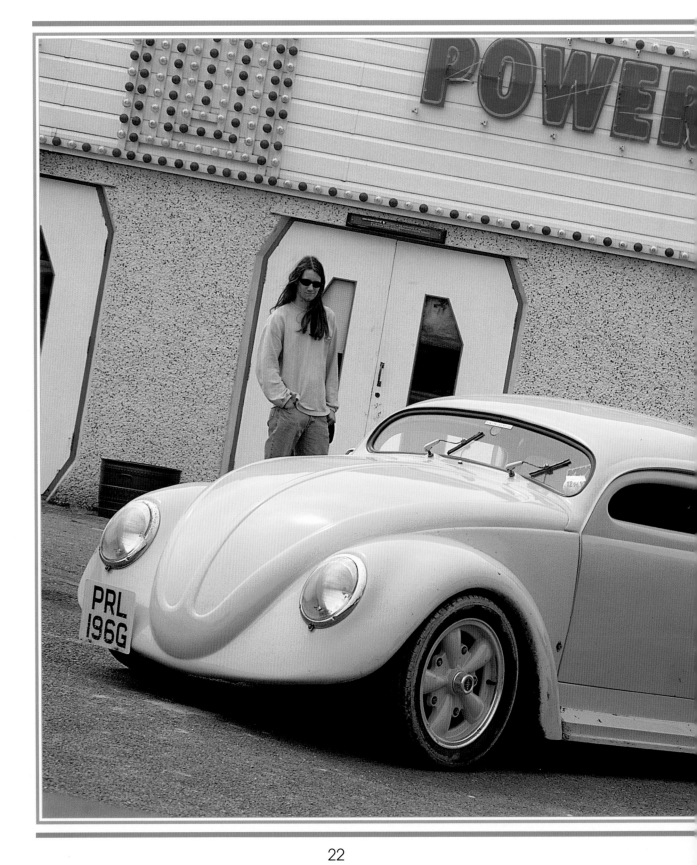

Fling open the doors and put the top down for the summer.

How low can you go? A Beetle to give you tunnel vision.

began a series of export sales drives which proved to be very successful; the Volkswagen was making an international name for itself.

The first variations on the people's car were being developed even before the Beetle's popularity was established. During 1939, Porsche was instructed to build a military version. This *Kubelwagen* was built on a reinforced version of the Beetle chassis, with upgraded suspension and an engine of larger capacity. There were no concessions to style - the vehicle had only to do its job, not look attractive while doing so. About 50,000 were made during the course of the war, including half-tracks, training vehicles in the form of dummy tanks, and four-wheel-drive prototypes. The strangest variation was the *Schwimmwagen*, an amphibious vehicle capable of 50mph/80kph on land and 15mph/24kph in water. A total of 14,000 units were built.

Thirty years after the military *Kubelwagen*, a new VW of similar appearance was introduced, but with rather more peaceful aims in mind. The Type 181 had a removable canvas top and ribbed bodywork, and was known in the USA as 'The Thing.' It was designed as a fun car, although it was practical enough; some were even sold as military vehicles. Small numbers of another version, the Type 182, or 'Trekker,' were sold, too, and a beach car version with no doors and canvas sunshade top was later built at the Mexico plant.

The Beetle has often been the basis for utility vehicles. As early as 1947, Hebmuller built

What would Dr Porsche have thought? (Wizard panel van conversion).

police cars for VW. These had canvas hoods, and some examples had canvas doors, too. Papler converted VW saloons into police cars. The hoods were better fitting than those on the Hebmuller version, and the cars had the benefit of steel doors. Paplers were also quite popular with fire departments - finished in red, naturally, rather than the shade of dark green chosen by the German police. Austro-Tatra was also in the police car market, but its version was regarded as less well finished than the other two.

The Beetle as an ambulance is a difficult concept to grasp, but the firm of Miesen managed to build such vehicles. The stretcher patient was placed - accurately - on a swivelling platform, which was pushed along runners until it was halfway through the passenger door, when it was swivelled carefully through 90 degrees. To make this remarkable shoe-horning exercise possible, the seats were specially designed to fold flat, with the rear backrest made in two sections so that a passenger could travel with the patient. The door was also altered so that it folded back on its hinges for better access.

One of Dr Nordhoff's first moves on assuming command at Wolfsburg was to plan the introduction of a Volkswagen cabriolet. He commissioned the Karmann and Hebmuller companies to produce prototypes. The Hebmuller car was of stunning appearance, a two-seater with a distinctive rear engine cover which was very similar in shape to the front bonnet. Although it was the more conventionally shaped Karmann that would go into full production, the two cars were launched alongside each other as alternative options: a two-seater and a four-seater. While both cars made a good start, however, the Hebmuller company suffered a serious factory fire

Not for people who get car-sick: turquoise convertible with seats, panels and dash upholstered in magenta leather with co-ordinated piping.

Now this looks like a nice, ordinary, rust-free Beetle. It will stay that way, too, because it has a fibreglass bodyshell.

Let's have three cheers for the car that started all this.

from which it never recovered. The company was liquidated in 1952, with only 700 cars ever built. But the Hebmuller shape was an ideal one for that 'custom' look, and an Australian manufacturer was producing Hebmuller-style body kits until quite recently, so there's still a chance of seeing a Hebmuller Beetle about.

There were other splendid Beetle cabriolets on the roads. Rometsch made a stylish open-top from 1950, with very sleek lines indeed, and also built coupé versions, later models of which were fitted with a wrap-around rear screen. The cars were redesigned in 1957 with transatlantic styling, and were generally considered attractive but less stylish than the originals. Rometsch also built a four-door Beetle taxi, with extra rear-hinged rear doors for passenger comfort.

Dannenhauser & Stauss

With pristine paint and a few chrome touches the real thing can look great, too.

made an attractive cabriolet which resembled the Porsche 356 in shape. The firm had no direct link with VW, and either bought base vehicles from dealers or converted customers' own cars. A very few coupés were built to special order, too.

From 1952, Stoll produced a five-windowed Beetle-based coupé. In 1949 the Swiss Beutler company introduced its first Beetle variation, with a removable Plexiglass roof panel. Five years later the company showed its Beetle-based coupé and cabriolet - elegant and quite unlike a Beetle in appearance. Beutler also built a variety of estate cars and vans which were not the most suitable forms for the Beetle due to lack of usable load space and that space-stealing engine fan.

With its separate chassis, the Beetle was just ideal for these special treatments. Although not all the coachbuilders were able to buy chassis direct from the factory, the process of stripping down the base vehicles and reclothing them was relatively straightforward. Similar objectives, plus good availability of spare parts old and new, have ensured that the Beetle has remained one of the most sought-after cars for customisation to the present day.

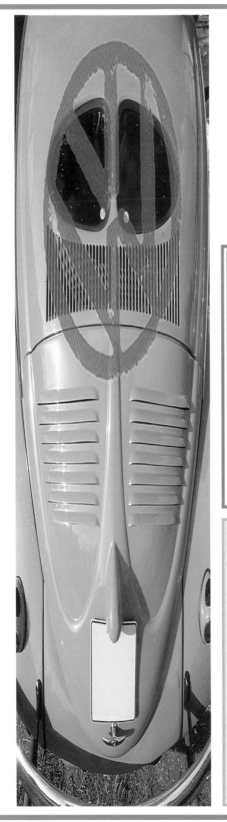

STREET MACHINES

Orange Speedster (56-JA-88)
Owners - Mario & Sandra De Trel

- Base model - basic 1300 automatic, 1976
- Engine - 1600cc, 36mm Weber Carb, K&N air filter, electronic ignition with Bosch 009 distributor and splitfire plugs
- Transmission - 1303S
- Exhaust - EMPI Monza 4 TIP
- Shocks - front Koni gas, rear stock
- Wheels - Borbet C alloys with Continental tyres
- Brakes - rear drums, front discs

Speedster kit and rear glass fibre wings by Wizard. Wide front and rear wings, lowered window. Some parts gold-plated. Pioneer stereo with 2x400watt, 2x180watt, 1x150watt speakers. Lowered, with adjustable front beam and a one split negative drop at the rear, chromed shock arms at the front. Underside painted black, with axles in yellow. Neon lights under side steps. Rear red lamps lenses with blue dots. Hand-made interior with wooden steering wheel rim and gearknob.

The Cal-look Beetle has become so widespread that the uninformed might assume these cars are factory-produced models in their own right. In truth, the first 'Cals' took to the roads in the mid-1960s, in the USA, naturally, although their popularity soon spread to wherever Beetles and their owners were to be found. Beetle drag racing was already gaining ground, and it was only a matter of time before that look - the lowered stance, beefed-up engine and lack of trim - found its way onto the streets.

The classic Cal-look today will be a one-off. Conforming to the basics of the style, it will have enough individuality to personalise it, but not so much that it starts to look fussy. The wheels will probably be custom, possibly courtesy of the Porsche 911, unless this is Cal-on-a-budget, in which case the standard items will be colour-keyed. Chrome has to go: most Cals have none at all. If any remains, it will be a feature - hubcaps, for example - but no showy bits and pieces are tolerated. A smooth, clean line is the aim; consequently, the pre-1968 sloping headlamps are more popular than later ones (fitting older wings on a car of later date can cause problems as they are not instantly interchangeable).

Cals come in every colour under the sun. Although early convention dictated a single colour (and red was the colour of choice), the Cals of today are much more adventurous. Deep pastels are a favourite, while dramatic colour schemes and interest-ing graphics are becoming ever more popular. Another well-liked Cal modification is 'Frenching' - rear lights and indicators are recessed into the body panel, either set into a piece of steel tubing or, in the case of rear light clusters, the original housings are reversed. On the inside of the car, a great deal of freedom of expression is possible. Some owners will choose a vast array of Porsche-style instruments on a dash crowded with goodies; others will go for a plain, unadorned dash with only a speedo. The overall effect, though, is of simplicity and style - a style that has stood the test of time with only minor changes of approach.

The essence of the 'Wizard' is a purpose-built bodyshell made of heavy-duty glassfibre, mounted on a reinforced Beetle chassis. The big advantage, from the bodywork point of view, is obvious - a rust-free Beetle! The first Wizard was built in 1980 by Chris Boyle, and was originally named the EDV (Every Day Vehicle) Super Coupé. The name soon changed to 'Wizards of Rods', then just 'Wizard.' A Roadster version followed, then the Beetle Van, and then the very first 'Windjammer,' complete with roll-bar and detachable hardtop.

In 1986 Chris sold the Roadster and Windjammer moulds and accessories to Peter Cheeseman, an expert in plastic and glassfibre technology and a Beetle fan of long standing. Three years later, the remaining Beetle kits followed suit, bringing all the Wizard products back under one roof. Peter soon extended the range to three Roadster versions - economy, Cal-look and four-seater convertible - plus the coupé, van, and a revised Windjammer.

In 1991, Peter decided to go one stage further and develop a saloon-style Beetle bodyshell in glassfibre. Unlike the Roadster body, which could be made in two pieces, the saloon body had to be constructed in one, which presented a whole new set of challenges to John Chapman at Fibretech.

Construction of the shell takes up to three days. The result is a light but sturdy reproduction of the Beetle bodyshape - roof, front and rear outer body sections and sills. There are only minor differences in style (no rain gutters, and the grille beneath the rear window is a dummy). To compensate for the loss of the air-intake, there is a special built-in duct to draw air from the area over the gearbox. Front and rear bulkheads, which have been formed separately, are bonded into the body and the whole is then ready to be fixed to a steel Beetle chassis, which will have been inspected and overhauled and, if necessary, the old floorpans replaced with new. A reinforcing steel subframe is also fitted at the same time as the body: it gives the necessary rigidity, supports the dashboard and steering column, and incorporates fixings for seatbelts.

Deficiencies in the original design can be improved upon in Wizard form. The heating system is refined with the aid of insulation material packed

There are a couple of little bugs inside, but they don't need ironing out.

Wizard-based Speedster shows off its 1600 engine.

56-JA-88

Three years of hard work on the part of Mario de Trel and his uncle went into this Speedster, finished - down to its gold-plated handles - just in time for Mario and Sandra to go to their wedding

into the sills as this helps to retain the heat in the ducting pipes. The one-piece dashboard offers almost unlimited potential for a personal selection of dials, gauges, instruments and accessories.

The finished Beetle weighs approximately the same as a standard, steel-bodied Beetle - and it will stay weighing the same, too, as no bits of bodywork will rust away!

The Wizard kits have formed the basis for many an imaginative conversion over the years. Not everyone will start and end with their Wizard kit in original form - Peter Cheeseman is able to recognise Wizard elements in weird and wonderful customisations from all over the world. A fully chromed engine has a see-through perspex engine lid to show it off. A massive sound system fills every available interior space with equipment - and with sound. A Roadster is completely kitted out inside in pink leather ... the Beetle seems to offer unlimited scope for the imagination.

There are many clubs dedicated to Beetles such as these, members meet to talk and cruise - the main object of the exercise being, of course, to drive that Beetle. Whereas one customised Beetle will turn heads, several cruising together will really pull in the crowds!

John Oron's Speedster is called 'Naughty by Nature.' Based on a Wizard kit, it's finished, mouth-wateringly, in Mazda Raspberry metallic paint.

Where two or three passengers might have perched, sits a custom-built stereo system, which shines at night with a purple neon glow.

'Naughty by Nature' Speedster (NH-21-JL)

Owner - John Oron

• Base model - basic 1300, 1971 • Engine - 1835cc with dual Weber 36mm carbs from Alfa 33 • Exhaust - Kadron • Wheels - EMPI Lemmerz, with knock-offs • Brakes - front and rear drums • Interior - front sports seats from Ford Capri III 2.0S, upholstery and carpets by owner

Wizard Speedster kit with chopped top front screen and shortened wipers. Polyester running boards, front and rear wings. Rossi headlights, red 1200-type rear lights. Tinted windows, one-piece side windows. Shaved polyester dash with frenched-in meters. Rear seat replaced by speakerbox with two 12 inch MTX 'Blue Thunder' woofers, two Pioneer TSW60. Macrom-Pro two way speakers in doors. Gelhard Indy Amplifier. Special battery and gold connections. Purple neon lights in speaker box and around amp. Chromed engine parts and painted block. Colour - Mazda Raspberry Metallic

Here, later light units are used to good effect.

Outside the effect is very orange, with a little lemon and white. Inside the effect is reversed: white with subtle touches of colour.

The engine may be exposed and the hood may be down, but a good garage to work in, and to protect the finished article, is a high priority.

Older-style Beetle headlamp units are a more popular choice on custom Beetles than the modern variety.

Below & right : Although so much has been changed, the essential Beetle qualities remain: the oval rear window, engine aperture and rear light cluster shapes are all very sympathetic to the original.

Would anyone in the early days have expected the Beetle to appear in metallic paint, let alone lend itself to so many variations of shape and design?

BUGGIES & BAJA

4

The very earliest Buggies were really nothing more than a Beetle minus the bodywork: basically, a chassis with seats. They were made with nothing more stylish in mind than having fun on the beach, although it soon became clear that there was a market for a more refined vehicle in the same vein.

Usually built on a shortened floorpan and with fibreglass bodywork and proper roll-cage, the crude Buggy has evolved into a street-legal, stylish car with plenty of scope for individuality. Although there are plenty of buggies that go racing, many are built solely with fun, open-top motoring in mind. Atten-

From their off-road origins, Buggies have gradually evolved into chic, sophisticated good-lookers.

Fully protective rollover-bars are essential, just in case the unthinkable should happen.

tion to detail is of prime impor-
tance and, as the engine is
very much on display, it must
be as beautifully prepared
and presented as the rest of
the vehicle.

The Apal company of
Blegny, Belgium, began
manufacturing kits to trans-
form the humblest of Beetles
into Buggies in 1969. Apal had
previously manufactured VW

chassis-based coupés, For-
mula Vee cars, the VW 1300-
based Samtrack and Horizon
as well as a Renault-based
jeep and a Triumph Spitfire
replica. The Buggy kits fit the
Beetle chassis as is (the long
version of the Buggy, which
seats four), or a chassis shortened by almost 30cm (the
short version, which is a two-
plus-two). Aware of the pitfalls

*Opposite - Not all Buggies
are completely open to the
elements. This one has
doors, windows and
innovative louvres at the
rear for extra ventilation.*

Left and below - It's always good to see where you're going ... and to let others know where you came from.

50

Baja Beetles may not have the finesse of finish of some other conversion styles ...

... but there is a paint scheme of sorts here. It's just that Baja enthusiasts are not hardened Beetle purists.

of open-top fun motoring, all Apals come with rollover bars and heavy-duty anchorage for seatbelts. Great enthusiasts of the Porsche tradition, Apal also manufacture replica Porsche bodies in a variety of styles. Up to 1981, more than 5000 Apal bodies had been sold around the world, but, today, the company concentrates on the manufacture of luxury bathrooms.

The Baja style is as different to the smooth Cals as the well-known chalk and cheese

Left - Buggy engines are exposed, so action must be taken against mud and sand. Regular cleaning and attention are very important to keep everything looking good, and running smoothly.

Scorching summer day, warm breeze, hot Buggy. (Apal 2000 with 1500cc engine).

Despite their origins. Buggies are not crude. Inside they can be comfortable, even luxurious - it's a personal choice.

Mauve Apal 2000 Buggy with 1200cc engine and yellow Apal L4000 1835cc engine.

relationship. Baja is so called because the style is similar in appearance to the Bugs raced in the Baja 1000 mile off-road race.

The main features of the Baja style are raised suspension, wide wheels, tube steel bumpers and chopped fibreglass wings, usually with beefed-up running gear as well. Baja enthusiasts are proud of their cars and come in for a good deal of criticism from those Volkswagen purists who feel that the only worthwhile Beetle is one with that 'fresh from Wolfsburg' look. In truth, though, some of those original Beetle characteristics are just what make the cars suitable for the off-road Baja-style treatment. Having the engine directly over the rear wheels makes for excellent traction, and the suspension has the kind of give that copes well with difficult terrain so the Baja can take on many a four-wheel-drive vehicle without shame. There are fewer parts than in a water-cooled car, and therefore less to go wrong, which is particularly important out in the Baja's natural desert habitat, where garages are few and far between. What the Baja enthusiasts love about their cars is that they are rugged and reliable, not too expensive to maintain, and - most important of all - tremendous fun to drive.

The Baja was built for off-road conditions - the rougher it gets, the better it likes it.

Another Apal variation: the Jet is a later form of the Apal Buggy.

Ferrari Testarossa-sided Buggy (overleaf)

Owner - Rudy Bylsma

• Base model - Beetle, 1956 chassis
• Engine - 1835cc with 4x40mm Dellorto Carbs (one for each cylinder)
• Brakes - rear drums from type II, front 1303S disks

'Testarossa' sides are not purely cosmetic, but are real air scoops, the left side cools notorious number three cylinder and the right side assists the oil cooler

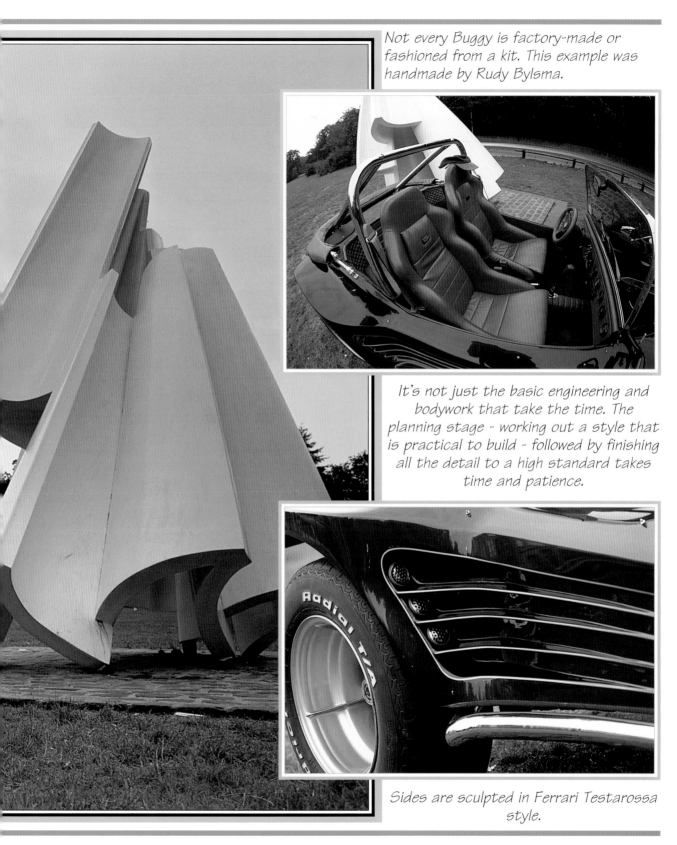

Not every Buggy is factory-made or fashioned from a kit. This example was handmade by Rudy Bylsma.

It's not just the basic engineering and bodywork that take the time. The planning stage - working out a style that is practical to build - followed by finishing all the detail to a high standard takes time and patience.

Sides are sculpted in Ferrari Testarossa style.

Apal Buggy

Polyester body kits for VW Beetle

Short (Kort) - Beetle wheelbase shortened by 27.3cm. Two-plus-two seater.
Long (Lang) - Standard beetle wheelbase. Four-seater

WHEN IS A BEETLE NOT A BEETLE?

The aim of all the hard work is not always to restore a Beetle to its original shape, or fashion it to a newer-style. Some Beetles end up looking nothing like the originals because they make a very practical base for the creation of something quite unexpected ...

Nick Slootweg spent many years as a service engineer for an agricultural machinery manufacturer, his travels taking him on many extended trips to the USA. Being an engineer and car enthusiast, Nick was very interested in the various types of kit-built cars he came across during his trips, one of his favourites being a Bugatti 35 replica. He looked carefully at how the car was made and dreamed of making one himself. However, money was tight and his job and other commitments left him almost no free time, so he had to be content to dream.

By 1985, however, Nick had a different job with the same company - one with more conventional working hours - and there was a little more money in the bank. He stopped thinking 'I could do that' and starting saying 'I'm

going to do it.' Then he went out and bought himself a 1970 Beetle with the chassis in excellent condition.

Nick believed that the next part of the exercise would be crucial to the project's success. He collected together all the leaflets, books and other information that he could find about Bugattis, and began to put together a specification for his car. He noted every measurement, from the obvious (like the size of the tyres and steering wheel), to the more specific (such as the height off the ground of the radiator and the exact cockpit dimensions).

He started the building work by narrowing the Beetle chassis, then reinforcing it. Next, he made the horseshoe-shaped radiator, the dashboard and the seats. Once these three items were correctly lined up, it was possible to shape the 1.5mm steel plate around it 'just by leaning on it,' says Nick, masterfully underplaying what must have been a rather intricate operation. The louvres were cut and shaped with a tool which Nick made especially for the purpose. Once the car was

Nick Slootweg's first Bugatti replica, complete with hand-fashioned, horseshoe-shaped radiator grille.

assembled, it had to be taken apart again and painted - in fact, Nick believes that each car he makes actually gets built at least three times!

When Nick says he made a car, he means just that. He made the eight-spoke Bugatti wheels, the four-spoke steering wheel, the leather seats, the dashboard (the bronze dials with the Bugatti logo), the Brooklands windows, the leather bonnet straps and the bronze specification plate. He also overhauled the 1200cc engine. He kept the VW wheelhubs, but the headlamps came courtesy of a Citroen 2CV and the horn from a Ford.

The bright red Bugatti took Nick three years to build. He is not allowed near a Bugatti meeting in his creation, but he's not worried. Of course, he is welcome at VW meets, and has taken many first prizes at shows and exhibitions. He also gets a huge amount of pleasure from driving it, and it has gained him many new friends.

Nick loves his red Bugatti 35, but he wanted something else - yes, these things can become an obsession, albeit a healthy one. He wanted something with a different character and decided on the Bugatti Brescia 27. Another Beetle was purchased. Nick shortened the chassis by 35mm, then turned the front axle the opposite way around, which effectively brought the wheelbase back to its original length but also changed the chassis to right-hand-drive. In truth, the operation was nowhere near as straightforward as it sounds; the car's whole geometry was

Left and opposite top - The Bugatti 35 replica is based around a 1970 Beetle chassis.

Left and next page - The second Bugatti, a convincing Brescia 23 replica.

Inside, the dash gets an authentic look, too.

changed and the logistics took some working out. The bodywork was made up in 1.5mm aluminium plate and stainless steel, with a traditional gearchange lever and handbrake outside the cockpit. Painted like its predecessor in original Bugatti Blue, this car also attracts attention wherever it goes.

Nick Slootweg gets as much satisfaction from building these cars as he does from driving them afterwards. This is why he decided to build something other than a Bugatti - a circa 1912 Mercer 35J Replica. He bought a Beetle, to use the front axle, the engine and the gearbox (the condition of the chassis was unimportant, this time, as Nick had decided to build his own). The 1200cc engine came in for a rather radical overhaul. It was transformed into a 600cc, two-cylinder unit by the removal of two pistons, two pushrods and two sets of valve rods. The holes in the crankcase were sealed, and the ignition system changed. The ignition timing and the choke are operated by levers on the steering wheel. The engine is put in back-to-front at the front end of the car, with the gearbox behind. He now had an engine with four reverse and one forward gear (or a car that ran backwards, depending on your point of view).

Chains were made which link the gearbox to an intermediate drive and thence, via further chains, to the rear axle, which Nick he made himself. The chain drives are fitted with eight adjustable oil drippers.

Mercedes double disc brakes are fitted. The petrol tank is, in reality, a 20-litre LPG tank. The headlamps are made from the cases of elderly voltmeters with reflectors fitted into them. In place of stoplights there is a stopshield. The car's engine, started with a handcrank, has both hand and foot operated throttles, and runs very smoothly indeed. Since the original Mercer was built in a refined age, another of its features should, perhaps, be described as a 'bovine excrement protection device,' from Oklahoma. Nick refers to it as the 'bullshit scraper,' and so shall we.

The car is painted in sandy yellow, co-ordinating beautifully with the polished wooden detail. It has earned Best Car in Show prizes, and is great fun to drive. Nick is particularly proud of his 100-metre run at the VW Euro sprint trials, when he managed a spectacular time of thirty-two seconds, the competition managing only a 'shameful' eight or ten seconds!

And still no-one would believe there was a Beetle engine in there, somewhere!

Nick has paid great attention to detail with the Mercer replica - nothing has been overlooked.

The Mercer uses running gear from a Beetle on a chassis which Nick built himself.

With the Beetle engine placed at the front, a system of chains was necessary to drive the rear wheels.

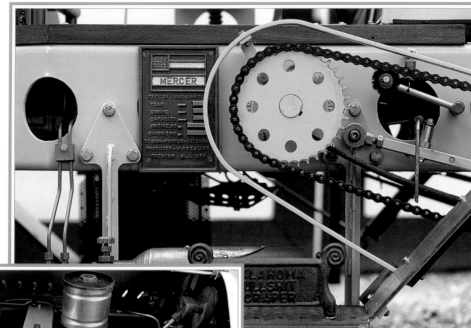

The Beetle engine - well, half of it, as it is now a 600cc, two-cylinder unit.

More of Nick's superbly detailed work.

Whatever Nick builds next, and whatever outside appearances may suggest to the contrary, it will probably have the guts of a Beetle in there somewhere.

Just like the old days: a starting handle to get the car - and the driver - going in the morning.

A PERSONAL
APPROACH

And if all these options leave you cold? You love your Volkswagen, for sure, but you would have to say, if pushed, that in its standard form you find it boring. Age and other drivers have not been kind to its bodywork, and the paint could do with some encouragement. You have neither the time, inclination or expertise to turn the thing into a Bugatti lookalike. You need the seats intact to take four backsides. You can't afford to shell out for a fibreglass shell. A Baja would be too bumpy, and a Buggy too cold. Fear not, there are plenty of options left. How many other cars do you know that would look really good with different colours on every panel? A Mercedes would look inappropriate that way, for certain; even a newer VW might look like a styling-cum-marketing exercise. A Beetle can take it. A Beetle expertly prepared and painted in a new, bright,

An aggressive sight in the rear-view mirror.

This lace-effect Beetle belongs to the good folk at the Wolfsburg museum.

There's nothing very unusual about this Beetle - except, perhaps, those windows on the far side ...

... getting into the back of a standard Beetle can be a pain - Wolfsburg should have made some this way!

From the side all becomes clear: it's a three-door Beetle.

Animal styling covers a multitude of bodywork sins. The extra seating works well - there must be room for four or five more yet.

Once seen, never forgotten - which is exactly the idea of a promotional Beetle with a bonnet on the bonnet.

Tasteful it ain't;
fun it certainly is -
Fred Flintstone-
style.

It never needs a
polish, just an
occasional trim.

No chrome, or very little, a smooth look in a beautiful pastel tone: the essence of the Cal-look, interpreted on a later Beetle gives a very modern look.

In the world of the customised VW, the Type 3 is not forgotten ...

... and the Karmann Ghia gets a piece of the action, too.

Raise your glasses for the one-and-only, the original Beetle - in all its forms.

all-over colour can look a million dollars.

Another alternative is to go daft. Those headlights look like eyes - so add eyelashes. Give it a smiling mouth, a nose, even a jaunty hat. Paint it with brush paint, and stick flower decals all over it (warning: this look clearly says 'I remember the 1960s and I'm over 40 years old'). Watch those old Herbie movies, and recreate your Beetle as a number 53 (but remember, it can't really fly). Cover your Beetle in fake fur - no more polishing, but regular grooming is required. Whatever you decide to do,

the Beetle can take it.

There are lots of models around that, over the years, have come out of the factory in many different versions. The Beetle's style stayed remarkably constant during its production life, but it lends itself to a surprising variety of customisations and personalisations. There are certainly more reincarnations of the Beetle than of most other cars. So many people love it; a huge number have, at some time in their lives, owned one - not many cars can claim a special edition to celebrate reaching the

twenty million mark.

With a plentiful supply of raw materials available, the market for 'new' Beetles has never been better. One advantage of the fibreglass body, for example, is that it enables the sound basics of a Beetle with rusted bodywork to be recycled, thus leaving older, classic examples - such as the oval-window model - for restoration without mutilation. Customisation is a thriving business. Individuality helps make motoring fun, and the Beetle knows all about that!

Photographer's postscript

All the photographs in this book were made on Fujichrome Velvia film, with Leica R6 cameras, and lenses ranging from 16mm fisheye to 560mm long focus. Since the other Family Albums on VW - Beetle and Bus - I have added a couple of zoom lenses, mainly to cut down on the weight, which was beginning to tell! But cameras, even the best, are only half the story, silent tools in the hands of a photographer. What of other hands? Hands that moved cars, picked up phones, got things done? It would be monstrous to take credit for the pictures in this book single-handedly, when they are the result of so many people's time and effort. The owners of wacky vehicles, the creators of wacky vehicles, are mentioned elsewhere in this book, but there are some whose devotion to the cause (often bordering on insanity, it must be said) makes them deserve to share some of the blame ...

John Oron, for instance, who drove me round Rotterdam for hours, so that I could look for locations, and arranged for his colleagues to bring their cars to railway stations, shopping precincts, council buildings and huge chunks of modern architecture. Not once did they flinch from driving up kerbs, driving on pavements, suffering the verbal abuse of all and sundry. And still they kept smiling.

I have known Raoul Verbeemen for a few years, and I am told that there was a time when he was considered normal, but it was so long ago that no one can actually remember when it was. He also downed tools, and drove me location hunting, arranged Buggies, a flower-power Beetle, and commandeered his daughter Eva as a somewhat eccentric (what else?) model. It's

obviously a family characteristic, as Eva coerced a friend, Vanessa Ramaekers, to join in and thereby accrue some of the guilt! Raoul's wife (and Eva's mother), Hilde, very sensibly would not take part, instead preferring to cook good food for us all on our return.

Etienne Mertens, escapee from the VW Beetle, and VW Bus Family Albums, came along to laugh at us and also to eat Hilde's food. His involvement was total, and perhaps more than any single person he should take the majority of blame for the contents of this book. He was also of immense help in arranging meetings and sessions with the Belgian Buggy Club. (Also, he makes coffee, lots and lots of coffee ...)

Gerard Wilke is another Family Album escapee, who has a veneer of normality but, who, with other members of the Kever Club Netherlands, provided me with access to all sorts of strange goings on, all of which involved Volkswagens, many of which involved mud, and some of which involved both in a great pit. Sad indeed!

At one of these off-road events I met Andrew Habrahen and Rudy Bylsma, both of whom had done strange things involving Testarossa-like ducts on the sides of their otherwise dissimilar vehicles. Naturally they were both barking mad, and (here's the giveaway) very keen to help me get 'unusual' photographs of their Beetles. Not only did Andrew obtain permission in advance for the use of a very nice background, he also persuaded Corine de Beer to be a model - a supermodel, in fact; again, quite mad. Rudy could only manage to fit in with my schedule by having the session in the evening. Unfortunately, Rudy was keen to talk about his car, and his lovely wife Marcolina was keen to feed us both, so that by the time we went to make pictures it was nearly dark, and the traffic had its lights on. We returned in total darkness!

It was in a muddy field in the Netherlands that I met Marco Orriens. He drives around, fighting a losing battle to look relatively normal, in a very strange car called a Regina. Unfortunately, space has prevented us featuring the cars from the Regina register, but they will be a part of our second volume. Marco introduced me to Nick Slootweg, whose cars tell you all you need to know (and more!) about Nick, except that Nick is a man who understands that photoshoots are driven by ninety per cent beer, and ten per cent inspiration, and he was determined to provide the ninety per cent!

Also in Holland, and therefore quite reasonably Gerard Wilke's fault, I met Bert Wolfink, who is not one for making cars from any sort of kit, oh no, but spends time making Ford-inspired shapes in the forms of car and trailer. He lives in the middle of a very large flat piece of Holland, next door to the stunningly lovely Nathalie van der Klok, whom he persuaded to come along on the shoot; good job, too.

I hope you all recover, though not too quickly. The world needs visionaries and I, for one, feel all the better for having worked with you all.